God is Our Keeper, Our Maker, Our Deliverer, Our Redeemer
Gospel Songs

Heavenly Realm Publishing
Houston, Texas

VERLER LAGRANGE ROBERTSON GORDON

This book is protected by the copyright laws of the United States. This book may not be copied or reprinted for commercial gain or profit. No part of this book may be reproduced, stored in a retrieval system, or transmitted by any means, electronic, mechanical, photocopying, recording, or otherwise, without written permission from the author and publisher.

Copyright © 2022 by, Verler Lagrange Robertson Gordon, God is Our Keeper, Our Maker, Our Deliverer, Our Redeemer Gospel Songs, *all rights reserved.*

Cover Design By: Heavenly Realm Publishing

Published by,
Heavenly Realm Publishing
1-866-216-0696

Visit our Website at:
www.heavenlyrealmpublishing.com
shop.heavenlyrealmpublishing.com

Printed in the United States of America

ISBN—13- 9781944383251 (softcover)

1. Religion: Music: *God is Our Keeper, Our Maker, Our Deliverer, Our Redeemer Gospel Songs/* Verler Lagrange Robertson Gordon. 2. Religion: Christian Ministry - General: *God is Our Keeper, Our Maker, Our Deliverer, Our Redeemer Gospel Songs/* Verler Lagrange Robertson Gordon. 3. Religion: Christian Ministry Music: *God is Our Keeper, Our Maker, Our Deliverer, Our Redeemer Gospel Songs/* Verler Lagrange Robertson Gordon.

This book is printed on acid free paper.

Scripture quotations from the New King James Version ®. Copyright © 1982 by Thomas Nelson. Used by permission. All rights reserved.

God is Our Keeper, Our Maker, Our Deliverer, Our Redeemer Gospel Songs

Verler LaGrange Robertson Gordon (2021)

Left Side: Marcus Boyd, Amiree Boyd, Ranada Gordon, Kay Kay Boyd
Right Side: Ranada and son Tarrell Gordon

Verler with family: Jackie Robertson, Micah Gordon (left), Lance Gordon, Camron Gordon (right)

God is Our Keeper,

Our Maker,

Our Deliverer,

Our Redeemer.

TABLE OF CONTENTS

Foreword 12
Dedication 15
I See Miracles 16
Worship in Gratitude 17
Jesus is The Light of the World 18
You are Beautiful 19
Let the Church Say – Amen 20
Whatever it Takes 21
I Wanta Feel the Power 22
Take Me to the Cross 23
Holy Ghost Power 24
Praise, Where Your Help Come From 25
You Are the Strong Name 26
Gospel Songs From: *John the Revelator in the Beginning* 27
I've Got a Testimony 28
The Storms 29
I Made it Out Alright 30
I'm Walking in Integrity 31
Hold on and Don't Let Go! 32
Jesus!! 33
In His Sanctuary 34
In My Life 35
Lord, Do it for Me 36
Glory Unto the Lord 37
Joy to the Church 38

Table of Contents

Thank You God! 39
He Delivered Me 40
He Loves Me 41
Give God Praise 42
On the Mountain Top 43
In Remembrance 44
I'm Better Because of Him 45
His Attributes 46
I'm So in Love with Jesus 47
Never Leave Me 48
When We Pray, Things Happen 49
Christ in Me 50
Walking in Victory 51
All the Congregation 52
You Forgave Me 53
I've Already Won 54
I Trust in You Lord 55
I Can Do All Things 56
Be Encourage 57
I'm Coming Out 58
I Learn to Lean on Jesus 59
Lord, I Wanta See Your Son - Jesus 60
I Walk in His Salvation 61
God is Love 62
He is Worthy 63
When We Get to Heaven 64
It Was the Blood 65
Praise Him for Who He Is 66

Table of Contents

I'm Thinking of You, Lord 67
Jesus is the Christ 68
All the Glory Belongs to Him 69
I'm Walking in the Favor of God 70
Wait on the Lord 71
Seasoned with Grace 72
I've Been Change 73
I Need You Lord 74
Cover Me Up, God 75
Is in My Heart 76
My Guilt and Shame is Gone 77
I am an Overcomer 78
His Glory 79
Judgement Belongs to God 80
Together 81
God is in Control 82
This is Christ Jesus 83
Jesus, You Been So Good to Me 84
The Joy of the Lord is My Strength 85
At the Mention of the Name 86
I Love to Praise Him 87
I Look to You Lord Jesus 88
I'm Holding On 89
I Thank God for Grace 90
He Saved Me 91
Where Are You Lord? 92
You've Changed My Life 93
Like David Did It 94

Table of Contents

I'm Free 95
I'm Ready for My Blessing 96
King of King and Lord of Lord 97
Some Thru the Water—Some Thru the Fire 98
Be Encourage 99
He is The Healer 100
One Parent World Biography 101
Family Collage 104
Acknowledgements 112
Meet the Author 114

FOREWORD

Oh, give thanks to the LORD!
Call upon His name;
Make known His deeds among the peoples!
Sing to Him, sing psalms to Him;
Talk of all His wondrous works!
(1 Chronicles 16:8-9 NKJV)

It is my pleasure to foreword this song book, "God Is Our Keeper, Our Maker, Our Deliverer, Our Redeemer;" not just because it was written by my sister, but because I know that every word in this book was written by the inspiration of the Holy Spirit. Before I go into the accomplishment of this book, I will tell you about my sister's morals. First, if there is anyone who shows gratitude to others; it would be Verler. Honesty is an attribute of hers. She is truthful and sincere. She is kind-hearted and will give you her last. She considers others and treat others the way she would like to be treated. Verler walks in integrity and sticks to her morals and ethical principles which she learned as a young girl growing up in a Catholic family background. She values truth and loves the Word of God.

Verler began to put this book together when the number "**54**" kept popping up on her clock or watch. One day I received a call from her expressing her concern about constantly seeing the number "**54**." I immediately told her to read **Psalm 54**, and much to my surprise she reminded me that she was born in **1954**. She started to read Psalm 54

Foreword

not knowing what was to be transpired. As she read Psalm 54 things began to work in her favor. Then, one night, she was roused by the Holy Spirit. She first was given a title. She wrote it. The next day, she wrote a song under the same inspiration of the Holy Spirit, to fit the title from the previous night. This is the way all her songs originated. From the first to the last, they were all inspired by the Spirit of God.

I pray that this song book will be a blessing to all who read it. Whatever your need may be, as you read each song, I pray your needs be met. Oh yes, another characteristic of my sister is love. For **God is love** (1 John 4:8) and you will see Him in every one of these songs.

Maranatha ~Our Lord has come~
Minister Dorothy L. James, RN

Foreword

Psalm 54 (NKJV)

1 Save me, O God, by Your name,
And vindicate me by Your strength.

2 Hear my prayer, O God;
Give ear to the words of my mouth.

3 For strangers have risen up against me,
And oppressors have sought after my life;
They have not set God before them. Selah

4 Behold, God is my helper;
The Lord is with those who uphold my life.

5 He will repay my enemies for their evil.
Cut them off in Your truth.

6 I will freely sacrifice to You;
I will praise Your name, O LORD, for it is good.

7 For He has delivered me out of all trouble;
And my eye has seen its desire upon my enemies.

DEDICATION

I will praise You with my whole heart;
Before the gods I will sing praises to You.
Psalm 138:1 (NKJV)

I dedicate this song book to my blind sister the late Helene LaGrange Wright. Though Helene was blind, she could see; she experienced the rhythm of the world through music. Helene understood that music is of the heart, a vibration of the heartbeats of spiritual songbirds. Helene had the voice of an angel and was truly an inspiration to me. Her favorite song was "He's an on Time God."

...He may not come when you want him
But he'll
Be there right on time
I'll tell you
He's an on-time God, yes he is...

Dorothy "Dottie" Peoples

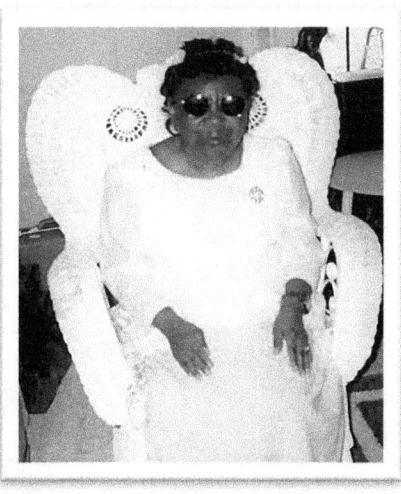

I See Miracles

If you believe in something, strong enough, it will come to pass.
I believe, you will see, it will come to pass.
I see miracles,
- People are being saved.
- They are being healed.
- Many are being set free.

I see miracles all about, let's not hide out.
Come out from among them;
Be ye separate says the Lord;
Touch not the unclean thing
And God say he will give you rest,
And many blessings.
I see miracles.

Sunday, 12/22/2019

Worship in Gratitude

I worship, I worship you.
Thank you for your grace you have bestowed to me, and the joy it gives me and I'm grateful to you Lord.
Worship in gratitude.
- Amen & Amen.
As we lift our hands in worship;
Worship in gratitude.
I thank the Lord as we worship in praise and raise our voices to the most High God.
His name is Jesus.
His name is Jesus.
We worship in gratitude.
Thanks

Monday, 12/23/2019

Jesus is the Light of the World

We must follow the light.
We must keep it in sight.
We must follow the light.
That good and wonderful light.
Yes, yes, Jesus is the light of the world.
He is our gift; we must be righteous in our life.
- Follow the light
- Follow the light
- Follow the light

Jesus is the light
- He's Alpha
- He's Omega.
- He's the beginning and the end.

Jesus is the light of the world.

Tuesday, 12/24/2019

You Are Beautiful

Jesus I'm beautiful in you.
Where there is illness I see health;
Where there is poverty I see wealth.
Jesus I'm in you; you are beautiful; and you love me
You are a strong tower in my weakest hour.
Jesus you are my savior;
I have good behavior; no hate, no strife, no malice, no envy, no pity.
You are beautiful. Full of love.
You are beautiful. Full of love.

Wednesday, 1/1/2020

Let the Church Say Amen

God has spoken, let the church say amen.
Lift your hands wherever you are;
Let the whole church say amen.
When your dream is about to die,
Say amen, amen, amen, say amen.
Keep it alive, it will come true.
God has spoken; let the church say amen.
Amen, amen, amen, -let the believers say amen.
Let the church say amen.

Friday, 1/3/2020

Whatever It Takes

Whatever it takes, I'm all in.
If it takes deliverance or a moment of silence;
I'm all in.
If it brings joy, peace and forbearance, I'm all in it.
Whatever it takes; God is going to open the window of Heaven and pour me out a Blessing which I have no room to contain.
Whatever it takes I am ready.
I'm all ready. I'm all ready. I'm all ready.
Whatever it takes. I'm all In.

Friday, 1/3/2020

I Wanta Feel the Power

I wanta feel the Power;
Power of the Holy Ghost.
Holy Ghost Power, Are you listening – Can you hear me?
I wanta feel the power – power of the Holy Ghost.
Wave your hands, look around and just stand and shout.
Dance and Romance in Jesus.
Do you feel his presence? I mean for real – do you feel the power?
Power of the Holy Ghost.
Holy Ghost Power.
Holy Ghost Power.
Power of the Holy Ghost.

Friday, 8:00pm, 1/3/2020

Take Me to the Cross

Take me to the Cross, I don't have any loss.
I found the Love of Jesus at the Cross.
God knows where I'm going; He Knows the way is to the cross.
Repentance is at the cross.
Take me to the cross.
Thank you Lord; thank you Lord.
We're no longer lost.
He died on the cross that we might find salvation.
Take me to the cross.
To be saved is at the cross.
Take me to the cross – to the cross.

Saturday, 1:54pm, 1/4/2020

Holy Ghost Power

The Lord saved me with his Holy Ghost power.
He saved me—he saved me.
You can't be saved without the Holy Ghost power.
Salvation is about the Father, Son and the Holy Ghost.
When we shout we move in the Holy Ghost power.
When we dance we clap in the Holy Ghost power;
The Holy Ghost power; the Holy Ghost power.
Come on gang, dance! Come on gang, sing!
Jesus gave us power.
Power in the Holy Ghost.
Holy Ghost Power. Power.

Saturday, 9:30am, 1/4/2020

Praise, Where Your Help Come From

Praise him in the morning, praise him at noon, praise in the evening too.

Your help come from praising Jesus at all times.

Don't be silent, don't be quiet;

Praise him, your help come from the Lord; Praise him.

Worship is in praise. Miracles is in Praise.

Deliverance is in Praise. Where your help comes from?

It is in your Praise.

Praise him!

Praise him!

Saturday, 4:30pm, 1/4/2020

You Are the Strong Name

Jesus you are the strong name.

The righteous run into it and they are safe.

You are strength to the meadows and rivers.

You bless the soldiers a far and will soon bring them near.

The United States may go to war;

Jesus is in it all the same.

You are the strong name.

May the United States stand tall.

Glory to all the men on the wall

They are coming Home safe.

Jesus, you are the strong name.

Tuesday, 8:45pm, 1/7/2020

Gospel Song from:
John the Revelator in the Beginning

In the beginning was the word and the word was with God.

The same was in the beginning with God.

All things were made by him; and without him was not anything made, that was made.

In him was life; and the life was the light of men.

And the light shines in the darkness;

And the darkness comprehended it not.

In the beginning, and now the light shines all over the world,

--- forever & forever

Tuesday, 1/7/2020

I've Got a Testimony

I look back over my life; I think things over; I got a testimony.

God has been good to me.

I got a testimony; I can truly say that I've been bless.

He picked me up; he put me on higher ground.

He woke me up this morning;

He picked me up and turn me around.

I can truly say that I've Been Bless.

I've got a testimony. I've got a testimony.

God has been good to me.

Wednesday, 1/8/2020

The Storms

The storms keep raging in my life.
Sometimes I can't tell the night from the day. ----
I say the Lord has answer prayers before today.
I pray the Lord my soul to keep.
O' the storms keep raging in my life.
He answers all prayers; so I know my storms are going to cease.
I'm at ease when I know he hears me.
Thank you Father, thank you for the Storms of life.
We go through and come out.
The storms – oh – the Storms Have Ceased.

Wednesday, 1/8/2020

I Made it Out Alright

Knowing God, I made it out alright.
Walking with him was my delight.
Ever since I met him I haven't been the same.
I –I – made it – I made it- out alright.
The day I made a way in Christ serving him is all I wanted to do.
I made it – I made it – I made it out alright.
We need you God, we couldn't make it without you.
Like wrong can't make a right
I made it out alright – alright – alright.

Wednesday, 1/8/2020

I'm Walking on Integrity

To be honest, integrity is my Goal.

Mom scold me about it long enough.

Yes, Jesus showed me honesty.

Now, I walk in integrity.

Ever since I've given my life to Christ I've been walking in integrity.

I walk It –

I Talk It –

I Live It –

The truth is, is my time, is my time to share and be honest with my peers about the true word of God.

I'm walking in integrity.

I'm walking in integrity.

Wednesday, 1/8/2020

Hold on and Don't Let Go!

Hold on and Don't Let go, hold on to God promises.
His Word is forever settled in Heaven.
I need you Lord, Right now. Oh how I need you, Right now.
Jesus, I'm holding on and I won't let go.
Hold on, Hold on, your gift is coming.
Everything is gonna' be alright.
Hold on and don't Let go.
He promise to see you through.
He's your friend and he won't let you go.
Jesus says hold on, hold on, hold on.
And don't let Go.

Wednesday, 1/8/2020

Jesus!!

Our father who art in Heaven.
Jesus, my Jesus. Hallowed be thy Name.
Thy name Jesus. Thy Kingdom Come-Jesus.
Thy will be done on earth – Jesus.
Father, God, your son Jesus lives within me.
I see my life changing as I sing this prayer to you. – Jesus.
Glory be to the father and to the son and to the Holy Ghost.
The Son, name is Jesus.
He watches over us.
He Saves Us; He Redeems us; He Sanctifies us.
Lord Jesus – Amen and Amen

Wednesday, 1:00pm, 1/8/2020

In His Sanctuary

Honor and majesty are before him;
strength and beauty are in "His Sanctuary."
The born – again Believers are in "His Sanctuary."
Retrievers are in "His Sanctuary."
The Holy Spirit lives within them.
They worship aloud in "His Sanctuary;" allowing Jesus to say yes.
When Jesus say yes nobody can say no.
Worship the almighty King; In "His sanctuary"
In His, In His, In "His Sanctuary."
Jesus is His Name.

Wednesday, 3:18pm, 1/8/2020

In My Life

I've got sunshine in my Life today.

The time is ticking and I'm a witness to His Glory in my life.

As I write these songs, I Know the Lord is on my side, yes, yes, He is in my life.

I know he is on my side.

The Lord is always on time, he has brought holiness in my life.

My children are my happiness; my sisters and my brothers are Loved in my Life.

I've got the Lord In my Life.

Wednesday, 1/8/2020

Lord Do it For Me

I will only leave this land as I take the stand
to depart headed for Heaven.
Lord, do it for me.
As I become a stewardess of your word, help me to study diligently;
Lord, do it for me.
It's going to be a brighter day when I see your
Son split the eastern Skies.
Lord, do it for me.
You don't Know how I want to be sure I'm headed for Heaven.
I won't stop seeking and receiving your Grace.
Lord, Lord do it for me, for me.

Wednesday, 4:18pm, 1/8/2020

Glory Unto the Lord

God is in the glory of the righteous.

The church shall praise him. Eph 3:21

His Glory is upon them. Glory unto the Lord.

The world shall glorify the Lord.

People of the north and South, east and west they will do their best worship.

Glory unto the lord; Glory; Glory.

Jesus is not forgotten; his Glory fills the earth.

Jesus is Lord. Remember he died for us. 1 Peter 1:8

It's Joy unspeakable and full of Glory unto the Lord.

Keep the faith – oh Remember hold on – Keep the faith.

Thursday, 3:40pm, 1/9/2020

Joy to the Church

The Lord has brought Joy to the church.

Take this tip he has given Joy to their lips.

Sing unto the Almighty Lord.

It is Joy unspeakable and full of Glory.

The Church shall magnify the Lord.

Sing --- sing – Joy – Joy –to the Church.

Shout –- Shout – Shout – with a Joyous Spirit.

Let every heart prepare his song from heaven in the <u>air</u>; from nature everywhere.

Joy, Joy --- to the church.

Sing Saints – Sing – Joyful.

Friday, 11:25am, 1/10/2020

Thank You God!!

Thank you God for your Son Jesus.

How wonderful he is; The truth is he's marvelous, and gracious.

Thank you God.

Jesus, the Son of God is powerful and we will serve him forever.

Thank you God!

My Song to you God is thank you, thank you, thank you my father.

You are merciful and I believe in you.

Jesus is beautiful and I thank you for him.

Thank you God for your love in sending us your Son.

Thank you God.

Thank you!

Friday, 1/10/2020

He Delivered Me

He delivered me.

I'm stronger than I've ever been.

I'm better than some of them.

I'm so much wiser than before.

Yes, oh, yes he delivered me.

There I sit at his Throne because I know that he cares.

I look everywhere, because I Know that his spirit is there.

I'm so glad he has delivered me.

Yes, oh yes he has set me free.

His freedom allows me to sing this song.

Yes, oh, yes, I've Been Delivered.

Yes, oh, yes.

Friday, 6:54pm, 1/10/2020

He Loves Me

Jesus loves me.

I'm so glad that he loves me.

One more day I must say he still loves me.

I'm headed for home.

Heaven is my home.

I'm so glad he loves me.

I stand in homage of how his hand reaches out to me and my heart is open to him.

I'm so glad Jesus loves me. He loves me.

His word is forever new in my soul. Matt 25:21

When I get home, I could hear him say – Well done – thy Good and faithful servant – enter – into thou – Joy of the Lord.

He Loves me.

Saturday, 8:12am, 1/11/2020

Give God Praise

I am so in love; I am so in Love with you.
I am giving you praise.
You give me strength; that's why I praise you – you – you.
I Give God praise.
I thank you Father.
I am so in love; I am so in love with you.
I lift my voice as I give you praise.
Heaven hears me I sing.
I give God praise.
I am so in love with you.
I love you.
I love you –- I love you.

Monday, 1:54pm, 1/13/2020

On the Mountain Top

I heard him from the mountain top, I saw him in the valley.
It was there on the mountain top; I received his message.
My life has not been the same ever since; never the same.
I found the fountain of youth on Jesus' mountain top; I felt like his eagles, soaring in the sky.
On the mountain top.
Yes, he lives high above us.
On the mountain top.
On the mountain top.

Monday, 2:54pm, 1/13/2020

In Remembrance

Jesus say we must pray and do this remembrance of him.
We must fast and do this in remembrance of him.
When we receive the Spirit, we must do this in remembrance of him.
Jesus say we must watch, and we must do this in remembrance of him.
<u>Luke 22:19, 1 Cor 11:24</u>
His word says do it in remembrance of me.
In remembrance of me.
My Lord, Jesus, say remember Him, remember Him, remember Him.
I do this in remembrance of Him.

Monday, 2:35pm, 1/13/2020

I'm Better Because of Him

I would be sad without him.
I'm better because of Him.
The news is it would be bad without Him.
I wouldn't want to be without Him.
In everything, I need Him.
He helps me in all things.
I'm better because of Him.
I'm better than I've been before.
I'm stronger than I've ever been before.
I'm better because of Him; because of Him --
-- Better because of Him.

Monday, 4:54pm-5:07pm, 1/13/2020

His Attributes

My attitude is to serve the Lord, in all of his attributes.
I praise him for his excellent Mercy.
Praise him for his loving Kindness.
Praise Him! Praise Him! Praise Him!
His attributes of Peace, Love, Joy, and tender Mercy deserves our attention.
Let's Praise him and rejoice.
The Lord is great, and merciful to be praise.
His attributes deserve our praise ---
Praise Him! Praise Him! Praise Him!

Monday, 5:54pm, 1/13/2020

I'm So In Love with Jesus

I will serve you whole heartily.

I'm so in Love with you, Jesus.

I serve you because I love you.

I Bow my Head in reverence to you because I love you.

I love you.

I'm so in Love with Jesus.

When I wake up in the morning my dawn is I love you.

When I go to sleep at night my dusk is I love you.

I'm so in love with you.

I love you.

I love you.

Jesus.

Monday, 6:54pm, 1/13/2020

Never Leave Me

Jesus, never leave me nor never forsake me.
This song has come to me in the middle of the night;
I could never lose sight of how I feel this night.
You done so much for me, Jesus, never leave me. Never leave me.
Never leave me.
When I think I'm all alone, You never leave me.
Jesus, you are here with me.
Never leave me. Never leave me.
Jesus, Never leave me.
Stay with me – never leave me.

Monday, 9:54pm-10:13pm, 1/13/2020

When We Pray, Things Happen

When we pray, the stars begin to shine, full moon appear; problems disappear.
When we pray, things happen, and we must stay anointed to receive them.
Prayer changes things.
When we pray, things happen.
It takes away all our pains and today, I say it smooth all our doubt.
When we pray, things happen.
We can Kneel and pray the help is on the way.
I can stand and Clap my hands: thank God when we pray, Things Happen.

Tuesday, 5:54am-6:14am, 1/14/2020

Christ in Me

Christ in me the hope of Glory. 1 Pet 1:8

It is joy unspeakable and full of Glory.

Yes, yes, I'm glad Christ lives in me. Psalm 97:7

We must worship Him. If Christ be in you – you must worship Him and bow down. Psalm 95:6

I'm glad Christ is in me. I believe Jesus is the Christ; the Son of the Living God; the Son of the Living God.

He Lives in me; Christ in me, He dwells in my mortal Body.

Christ in me, I feel Swell.

Christ in me, the Hope of Glory.

Tuesday, 8:24am, 1/14/2020

Walking in Victory

I'm walking in victory.

I'm walking in peace.

God say He will Keep us in perfect peace whose mind is stayed upon him. Isa 29:9

I'm walking in Love. His word say Love your neighbor as yourself.

I'm walking in victory.

I'm walking in Joy.

Reach for joy, the meek shall increase their joy. Isa 29:9

I'm walking in Victory, God gonna' make a way.

Surely as I say to you.

I'm walking In Victory, stand on His promises.

He promises to give us Love, Peace, and Joy.

I'm walking in Victory. Yes, yes, I'm walking in Victory.

Yes, yes, I'm walking in Victory.

Tuesday, 8:54am-9:20am, 1/14/2020

All the Congregation

Let all the congregation say Amen. Neh 5:13

Say Amen, Say Amen.

Let all the people raise their voices.

Red, yellow, black or white, God loves everyone in his sight.

He will make it alright as we sing all night.

Let all the congregation say Amen.

Say Amen, Say Amen.

The people sang loud and let all the congregation say – Amen.

Ya ya Say Amen, Amen.

Tuesday, 9:54am-10:10am, 1/14/2020

You Forgave Me

I trust in God for forgiveness.

I'll keep on trusting God.

When the road ahead of me is rough and my mistakes are tough;

I am going to keep on trusting God.

Forgive me God;

I'm calling your name Jesus, for every mistake I make.

I know you've forgiven me.

You died on the cross for me.

Thank you father – Keep on forgiving me.

You stretched – out your arms for me.

You tied my sins on the cross.

You forgive me.

Thank you.

Tuesday, 2:54pm-3:15pm, 1/14/2020

I've Already Won

Because of the Name, Jesus I've already won.
Jesus say fight; Jesus say win.
Because of him, I've already won.
Is on top of a mountain, I've already climb.
Is in a valley, I've already claim.
If it is a game, I've already won.
Through Jesus all things are possible.
Our winnings are acknowledged and real.
Our reality by faith are already won.
Oh, uh, oh, uh, won, won, won, I've already won.

Tuesday, 3:42pm-3:54pm, 1/14/2020

I Trust in You, Lord

I trust in you Lord to make all things right.

Prayer changes things.

You give the Blind sight.

The lame to walk. The dumb to talk. The deaf to hear.

When we trust in you are near.

    - Come go with me. – Come go with me.

I trust you will see, the Lord is Almighty, he is worthy to be praise.

I trust in you, Lord.

Lord, I trust in you.

    - Come go with me – Come go with me.

<u>Isa 50:10</u>

Let us trust in the name of the Lord.

I trust in you, Lord.

Wednesday, 3:22pm-3:42pm, 1/15/2020

I Can Do All Things

I can do all things through Christ who strengthen me.
I gain possession when I make confession of who he really is.
My decision is to serve Him with everything I do.
I can do all things in truth before Christ.
<u>1 Tim 6:13</u>
I can do all things; I can, I can,
I stand by the anointing that comes from Christ.
With my hands lifted up; I confess that Christ makes me strong.
I can do all things;
I can do all things, through Christ who strengthens me.

Wednesday, 3:43pm-4:00pm, 1/15/2020

Be Encourage

Be encourage a change is going to come.
Christ has delivered us.
Be encourage, He has set us free.
He has redeemed us.
He has Kept us; be encourage ya- be encourage.
The Bible say – David – encourage himself.
So – be encourage.
Encourage yourself.
Look to the hills – from whence cometh thy help?
Thy help comes from the Lord.
Be In the mist ya ya – Be encourage.

Wednesday, 4:13pm-4:24pm, 1/15/2020

I'm Coming Out

I'm coming out without a doubt.
I call on the Lord; I can't live without the help of the Lord:
I'm coming out of <u>poverty</u>
I'm coming out of <u>sickness</u>
I'm coming out of <u>distress</u>
I'm coming out of <u>worry</u>
I'm coming out of <u>mistrust</u>
I'm coming out of <u>misery</u>
I lean not to my own understanding; but in every way I acknowledge Him.
The Lord is my Light and my Salvation;
The Lord is the Strength of my life. <u>Psalm 27:1</u>
I pray to Him.
Yes I'm coming out. I'm coming out.

Wednesday, 4:21pm-4:37pm, 1/15/2020

I Learn to Lean on Jesus

Learn to lean on Jesus.
You are my comforter.
My faith in you, Jesus is because I Know your Word.
I trust in your truth.
I learn to lean on you, Jesus.
I put my guilt and Shame on learning to accept your comfort, I will play no game.
The same Jesus who was there in the latter days is here for us today.
I learn to lean on you, Jesus.
I learn to lean on Jesus.
Lean on you, Jesus.

Tuesday, 3:10pm-3:20pm, 1/21/2020

Lord, I Wanta See Your Son -Jesus

Lord, I wanta See Your Son – Jesus
Jesus when are you coming Back?
When are you coming Back?
Lord, I wanta see your Son, Jesus.
We're waiting on you, Lord.
I'm living the best of life.
I'm waiting for you to test my life.
When I see you, Jesus the wait will be over.
Lord, I wanta see your Son, Jesus.
I'll say this is the day, that the Lord has made.
There will be Light in the shade.
Lord, I wanta See your Son, Jesus.

Tuesday, 3:24pm-3:39pm, 1/21/2020

I Walk in His Salvation

Salvation is the Key to living holy.

Holy is the name of Christ.

I walk His Salvation.

He saved me! He saved me!

I've been baptized.

I've got the Holy Ghost and fire and it's Keeping me alive.

I'm walking in His Salvation.

Christ has died, Christ is risen, and Christ will come again.

I'm walking in His Salvation.

In His Salvation; In His Salvation.

Tuesday, 4:10pm-4:25pm, 1/21/2020

God is Love

I'm in love with you,

I'm in love with me, because God is love, and I love God.

Yes, I love God and God is love.

Super Stars and Super Flys are sometimes mistaken Love.

Do they Know real love?

Are they blinded by their money?

Remember, God is love and they that worship him must worship him in spirit and truth.

Remember, God is love, worship your majesty.

God is love.

He is love.

Tuesday, 4:38pm-4:54pm, 1/21/2020

He is Worthy

Jesus is always Blessing me.
He is good to me.
He is worthy to be praise.
I sing and lift the name of Jesus high.
Now is the Season of mercy and grace.
He is worthy.
Jesus is always Blessing me; an abundance of riches.
He is worthy --- He is worthy.
Now is the season to call on his name cause He is worthy -- He is
Jesus is Worthy.
Worthy.

Tuesday, 8:54pm-9:03pm, 1/21/2020

When We Get to Heaven

When we get to Heaven, what a joyous day that will be.
The angels will be rejoicing.
God will be working it out for us.
There will be no turning back.
What a way that will be.
Walking the streets of Gold, walls of jasper and entering gates of pearl.
When we get to Heaven.
When we get to Heaven, what a joyous day that will be.
When the trumpet will sound, time will be no more.
When we get to Heaven.
Get to Heaven --- Amen

Wednesday, 8:54am-9:07am, 1/22/2020

It Was the Blood

It was the Blood that give me strength from day to day; it will never - never lose its power.
It was the Blood that Jesus shed way up on Calvary.
It was the Blood that we must apply to our life;
It will never lose its power.
Way up - way up on Calvary.
It was the Cross, he laid on to bring love and peace endurance forever.
It was the Blood he shed —
way up - way up on Calvary; on Calvary - on Calvary.

Wednesday, 9:12am-9:21am, 1/22/2020

Praise Him for Who He Is

He's been good, praise him for who He is.
He's been good to me.
Clap your hands; lift your voice, praise Him, praise Him.
Come bless the Lord, come bless the Lord.
Praise Him for who He is.
Praise His name, His Name is Jesus.
Praise Him for who He is.
Come bless the Lord. When your dreams are of no avail – He makes it real. So, praise Him for who He is.
Praise Jesus!
Praise Him!

Wednesday, 9:22am-9:32am, 1/22/2020

I'm Thinking of You Lord

My thoughts of always living happy and Holy, is in you, Lord.
I'm thinking of you, Lord.
When I talk, when I walk, when I sit, when I stand, you are the Great I Am, the Great I Am.
I'm thinking of you, Lord.
When I stumble and fall, I Know you will pick me up.
Yes yes - I'm thinking of you, Lord.
Your presence is here, Lord.
I'm thinking of you, Lord.

Wednesday, 9:35am-9:48am, 1/22/2020

Jesus Is the Christ

Bless his Holy Name.

Jesus is the Christ – the Son of the Living God.

Oh, bless his Holy Name – Jesus.

Trust in Him, and lean not to your own understanding; In all ways acknowledge Him, and He will direct your path.

Jesus is the Christ – the Son of the Living God.

He is – He is –

Jesus is our Keeper,

Jesus is our Maker,

Jesus is our Deliver,

Jesus is our Redeemer,

Jesus is the Christ – the Son of the Living God.

Wednesday, 10:00am-10:14am, 1/22/2020

All Glory Belong to Him

Glory be to the father, and to the son, and to the Holy Spirit; and as it was in the beginning is now, and ever shall be, World without end, Amen.
-- All the Glory belongs to Him.
The Glory, the Glory – yes – it belongs to the father; It belongs to Him.
Talk to Him, talk to Him right now.
-- for all the Glory belongs to Him.
Come to Him, Come to Him right now.
-- All the Glory belongs to Him.
Come and talk to the father right now – right now –

Thursday, 10:20am-10:30am, 1/23/2020

I'm Walking in the Favor of God

His Grace and Mercy has brought me this far.
I'm walking in the favor of God.
I'm taking step by step into his Kingdom.
Long live the King as I walk to His Throne.
I'll keep believing that God is near – so – oh so,
I'll keep walking – walking in his favor.
I'm walking in the favor of God.
When I get there, face to face, I'll Know that I've won the race.
I'm walking in the favor of God.
In His favor.

Thursday, 9:20am-9:28am, 1/23/2020

Wait on the Lord

I don't mind waiting on you Lord.
I know you're coming soon.
Soon and very soon we are going to see you, Lord.
We are waiting on you Lord.
Our spirit is waiting on you Lord.
We look forward for our Blessed Savior to return.
We're looking, we're watching, we're waiting –
Yes, yes, wait on the Lord. He will renew our strength as eagles.
Wait on the Lord.
Yes I say this day.
Wait on The Lord.

Thursday, 12:45pm-12:58pm, 1/23/2020

Seasoned with Grace

When we are seasoned with pain,
the Blood of Jesus will season us with Grace.
He took the pain in his hands and feet.
Oh, Jesus I receive your Grace.
It is by Grace we are saved, yet not of ourselves, it is a Gift of God.
Jesus is that Gift.
We are seasoned with His Grace.
I see great things; I see Blessings from this Grace.
It is our time to put away pain, and receive our breakthrough by His Grace.

Thursday, 2:22pm-2:28pm, 1/23/2020

I've Been Change

I follow you Spirit daily; thank God I've been change.

I interact with others faithfully; thank God I've been change.

My state of mind is not the same; yes, oh, yes, I've been change.

Now, I follow the will of God; thank God I've been change.

I move and beckon at his command, I've been change, I've been change.

Thank God almighty, to him be the Glory; I've been change, oh yes, oh yes, I've been change.

Friday, 6:00pm-6:12pm, 1/24/2020

I Need You Lord

When I wake up in the morning I need you.
I need you every hour of the day.
In every way – you make me feel brand new.
I would be blue if I didn't have you.
I need you, Lord.
I need you.
I need you like I need air to breathe.
It may not be fair to some, but we all need you, Lord.
All day long, I say I look for you to make away. I need you Lord.
I need you, Lord. I need you.

Friday, 6:15pm-6:21pm, 1/24/2020

Cover Me Up, God

Cover me up with your Grace.

Cover me up with your Love.

Cover me, cover me, cover me.

Here I am to worship you.

Here I am to bow down, cover me up with your Grace.

Cover me up with your Love.

You are wonderful, you are counselor, you are almighty God.

Cover me, cover me, cover me.

Here I am to worship you.

Cover me up God.

Cover me.

Saturday, 4:54pm-5:14pm, 1/25/2020

Is in My Heart

Jesus, is in my heart to Love someone who doesn't love me,
Because I got you in my heart.
Jesus, I can do for those who don't do for me.
Is in my heart to honor someone who don't deserve my honor,
Because I Honor you Lord.
Is in my heart to share my testimony with others because I wear the need to free your Word from my heart.
Is in my heart, Lord.

Monday, 1:54pm-2:00pm, 1/27/2020

My Guilt and Shame is Gone

As I awoken, I knew something was different.
I had a walk, a new talk, a new song on my heart.
I had no guilty or shameful feeling; my life had been renewed.
My guilt and shame is gone.
My attention was on a new day with a new way.
I face no guilt or shame after a careful nite of prayer.
God has taken my burden and shaken my thoughts, and
my guilt and shame is gone – gone – gone.

Tuesday, 10:22am-10:56am, 1/28/2020

I Am an Overcomer

I am an overcomer through Christ who strengthen me.
Oh, how I love Him so.
I have overcome temptations, and I've walk through my trials and tribulations.
Oh, how I love Him so.
I am an overcomer, an overcomer I am.
He's healed me and delivered me; oh, how I love Him so.
In Him will I trust never to be misunderstood; cause I am an overcomer.
-- An overcomer I am.

Monday, 2:54pm-3:07pm, 1/27/2020

His Glory

We can expect the Glory of God.

His Glory will fill the earth.

Above and beyond our calling is for more love.

His Glory will be astounding through our pastors and preachers.

Let the whole world be healed and set free; his Glory will seal the Church.

His Glory shall be seen upon us; and all his people shall see His light shine.

We can expect the Glory of God.

His Glory, His Glory -----

--- will fill the earth.

Monday, 2:30pm-2:45pm, 1/27/2020

Judgement Belongs to God

All Judgment belongs to God our father.

When we get to the golden gates of Heaven, then we'll Know we have met the Great Judge.

He will say well done or depart from me.

Ya – ya – Judgment belongs to God.

Will you be ready?

<u>1 Pet. 4:17</u>

for Judgment must begin at the house of God.

Is your house clean?

After this, the Judgment.

Judgment belongs to God.

Chose this day who you will serve.

Ya --- ya – who do you belong to.

Tuesday, 9:54am-10:22am, 1/28/2020

Together

I am not alone, it is you and me Lord.

Together we can do anything.

I choose to worship you. Without you I am nothing.

Together we can do something.

Some now, some later, and forever; Together we can do anything.

I choose to believe in you, that is why you are my everything.

Every morning when I wake up, I look to your daily Glory because, together we can do anything.

I am not alone, it is you and me Lord.

Together we can do everything.

Can do, can do, anything.

Amen and Amen

Sunday, 11:54pm, 2/2/2020

God is in Control

God is in control.
He controls every movement of our bodies.
When our eyes blink, is in him we can wink.
When we use our head, is in him we can think.
God is in control.
Every knee shall bow, every tongue shall confess at the sound of His name.
God is in control.
He controls every movement of our bodies.
When our ears will hear, he will appear.
When we move our fingers and clap our hands in worship; all his fans; we can rock and roll.
God is in control.
In Control—rock and roll.

Friday, 2/14/2020

This is Christ Jesus

This is Christ Jesus, the son of the Living God.

It's remaining to be seen, Jesus is the Christ; as he extends His dominion over all the earth.

This is Christ Jesus' magnificent work.

Glory be to God and to His Son Jesus.

This is Christ, the son of the Living God. Jesus is His Name.

Holding close to Him is all I want to do.

Living for Christ, I will never be without.

This is Christ Jesus, the son of the Living God.

I keep on obeying his earthly commands.

He extends His dominion over all the earth.

Jesus is the Christ the son of the Living God.

Friday, 6:54pm, 2/14/2020

Jesus, You Been So Good to Me

So good to me, so good to me; you've given me liberty.
So much freedom that I could see.
You brought me out without a doubt.
You gave me promises that I will never be without.
Jesus you been so good to me.
You made a way for me.
Every day and in every way.
Jesus, I love you. Thank you, Jesus.
So good to me; so good to me.
Jesus you been so good to me.

12/12/2019, 2:54pm

The Joy of the Lord is My Strength

I'm going to Keep on shouting;

I'm going to Keep on singing;

I'm going to Keep on giving;

The Joy of the Lord is my Strength.

I'm going to Keep on praising;

I'm going to Keep on praying;

I'm going to Keep on dancing;

The Joy of the Lord is my Strength.

I'm going to Keep on, Keeping on.

Yes—I'm happy, happy, happy.

I smile over many miles because I love the Lord.

The Joy of the Lord is my Strength.

I'm going to Keep on, Keeping on. Keep on, on, and on.

Friday, Valentine's Day, 2/14/2020

At the Mention of the Name

At the mention of the Name, Jesus, every knee shall bow, every tongue shall confess… Jesus. Jesus is the name of the Son of the Living God.
There is Faith at the Name of the living God.
There is Hope at the Name of the living God.
There is Healing at the Name of the living God.
There is Power at the Name of the Living God.
There is Deliverance at the Name of the Living God.
At the mention of the Name, Jesus, every knee shall bow, every tongue shall confess… Jesus.
Jesus is the name of the Son of the Living God—the Living God—Jesus is that Name.

Sunday, 2/16/2020, 12:54am-1:03am

I Love to Praise Him

I love to Praise you Jesus.

Praise Him in the morning; Praise Him at noon; Praise in the evening too.

I love to Praise Him. Praise Him; Praise Him.

Praise Him 'til the sun goes down.

Jesus say if you love me, Keep my commandments;

Praise Him, praise Him, come on let's Praise Him, Praise Him.

Praise Him in the temple, come on people praise Him. Praise Him.

I love to praise Him; All—all Day long.

Praise Him; Praise Him; All-Day long.

Praise Him; Praise Him.

Sunday, 2/16/2020, 1:54pm

I Look to You Lord Jesus

I look to you Lord for my comfort.
I look to you Lord for all my benefits.
Come let us adore you,
- Come let us be redeemed by you,
- Come let us be counseled by you.

I look to you Lord for my comfort.
I look to you Lord for all my benefits.
It is comfortable to walk and talk with you Lord.
I look to you, Lord to you Lord, In you I see your Glory;
I see my answer to every prayer in every way, every day.
I look to you, LORD.
I look to you, LORD.

Sunday, 2/16/2020, 2:40pm-2:54pm

I'm Holding On

You've made me mighty and strong, every day I live I'm holding on to your faith. My faith in God is not to let go.
         I'm holding on.........to my now
            holding on......to my present
               holding on......to my future
                  With You.

God, I'm believing in you to see me through. I serve a mighty God; I serve a great big God. I'm Holding on to His promises.
         I'm holding on.........to my deliverance
            holding on......to my healing
               holding on......to my freedom
                  in Him.

He has made me mighty and strong. My faith in God is not to let Go.
Holding on.

Tuesday, 2/18/2020, 3:54pm

I Thank God for Grace

I thank God for His Grace.
It was His Grace that brought me this far.
I'm in this race.
He has delivered me.
By His Grace I stand, and on
the other hand he keeps me,
and He won't let me go.
I thank God, I thank God, I thank God for His Grace.
I rest in His Arms and He brings out the best in me.
My heart beats at a steady pace as I run this race.
So, I thank God for His Grace.
Thank God. ...Thank God.

Tuesday, 2/18/2020, 8:54pm

He Saved Me

He saved me, He saved me, I've been baptized.
Salvation is of upmost importance.
The more we use the substance of Living for God; Baptism and holiness can be enjoyed.
He saved me, He saved me, I've been baptized.
Let me tell you....

> *Accept Jesus Christ as your personal*
> *Lord and Savior and you shall*
> *be saved. Confess with your mouth*
> *and believe in your heart*
> *that Jesus was raised from the dead;*
> *and you shall be saved.*

He saved me, He saved me, I've been baptized.
Salvation is of upmost importance.
He saved me, he can save You.

Wednesday, 2/19/2020, 11:10am

Where Are You Lord?

Where are you Lord?
You are here, you are there,
you are everywhere.
We need you Lord.
We find you at the altar.
There is no other way, but there.
There is no other place, but there.
At the Altar, at the altar, we ask, where are you Lord.
You are Lord my King, master of everything.
All creation ask for you, at the Altar they receive you.
Where are you Lord?
You are Lord my King,
master of everything.
All Creation ask for you, you Lord.

Friday, 2/21/2020, 7:34pm

You've Changed My Life

Aw...Aw...La...La...You've changed my life.
I'm not afraid to say, Jesus when you came into my life, I became a new creation.
Aw...Aw...La...La...You've changed my life.
The reason is I'm in a new season. The Glory of the Lord Jesus is my story.
Aw...Aw...La...La...You've changed my life.
Growing daily I'm pressing through. You've made a way, you've made a way, every day.
Aw...Aw...La...La...You've changed my life.
A new Creation I am in You.

Friday, 2/21/2020, 8:14pm

Like David Did It

David slewed the giant and knocked him out.
I send notice to my family when the enemy speaks negative into your life, knock him out; Like David Did it; he slewed the giant.
Gracefully your thoughts will align with the word of God; and you will be set free.
Knock him out, knock him Out, knock him out…Knock that devil out.
Like David did it, he knocked that giant out.
When the enemy tries to steal your Joy-- Knock him out!
When he tries to steal your Peace-- Knock him out!
Knock that Devil out!

Friday, 2/21/2020, 8:54pm

I'm Free

I once was bound, but now I'm free.
I'm free, I'm free,
I'm free from trials and tribulations.
I'll sing this to all nations.
I wave my hands, and I will stand up for Jesus.
He set me free; He set me free.
He met me in church a long time ago. He called me out.
I'm free; I'm free—oh—oh—yes, I'm free.
He been so good to me.
Jesus has given me liberty.
Thank God I'm free, I'm free, I'm free.
Yes! Yes! I'm Free!

Friday, 2/21/2020, 9:54pm

I'm Ready for My Blessing

My God is big, so strong and mighty.
I'm ready for my blessing.
God is my strength as I receive my blessing.
Thank God I'm blessed, I'm blessed, I'm blessed.
I'm ready for my blessing today.
When I woke up this morning, I was ready for my Grace, my Smile,
my new day in a brand-new way.
Yes, I'm ready for my Blessing.
I begin my day with talking to God,
I'm walking in His Victory.
Yes, oh yes, I'm always ready for my Blessing.

Saturday, 2/22/2020, 7:54am

King of King and Lord of Lord

He's King of King and Lord of Lord; He's King of Heaven above.
He's Lord of Love, to all.
He's King of King and Lord of Lord:
> Lamb of God and Light of the World.
> Armor of God and fight for the Old.

He's King of King and Lord of Lord:
He's Alpha and Omega, the beginning and the end, the first and the
Last, In Him; in everything.
King of King and Lord of Lord.
He's master of everything. He's King of Heaven above.
He's Lord of Love, to all.
He's King of King and he's Lord of Lord.

Saturday, 2/22/2020

Some Thru the Water Some Thru the Fire

I've been thru the water when I was baptized in Jesus Name,
So, I will not go thru the fire.
It is my desire to live for Him.
Some thru the water; some thru the fire.
It is my desire to live for Him.
I've been baptized. I'm blessed, I'm blessed.
I'm not going there—It's hot.
It's hot—Hell fire is hot;
Some thru the water; some thru the fire.
Get Baptize in Jesus Name.

Sunday, 2/23/2020, 8:30am

Be Encourage

Lift your head up high, you're not walking alone, so be encourage.
God is with you and I am too.
I sing because you're beautiful; I sing because you're wonderful.
This song is dedicated to the broken hearted.
I once was in that place myself.
Look up, it won't be rough.
Lift your head up high, you're not walking alone, so be encourage.
God is with you, and I am too.
I sing because you're beautiful; I sing because you're wonderful.
Fully beautify your hearts, beautify your thoughts.

Monday, 2/24/2020, 6:54pm

He is the Healer

Jesus is the Healer; there is no sorrow that he cannot heal.
There is no pain that he cannot heal; he is the healer.
He can heal any downfall you go through.
The battle is not yours, it's the Lord's.
Give it to him, He is the Healer.
He can heal any disease you may have.
Any sickness you may face can be trace to the healer.
You can be sure there's a cure.
Jesus is the healer.
He paid the price on the old rugged cross.
In Him there is no loss.
He is our healer.
Our Healer……Our Healer……Our Healer.

Monday, 2/24/2020, 7:54pm

One Parent World Biography

It takes two, but a one parent world. Come, and let us examine this statement. Why, two is for God to explain, and why one is for us to remain faithful? Our books contain information about how we were created. The Bible states facts about Adam first man, from his rib a woman, Eve was formed. In the book of Genesis, chapter 2:7, man was given the breath of life, and Adam then Eve became the first two with our marriage union.

What does marriage mean in God's eyes? Two people coming together in respect to the sex act and having the wife conceive and bore a child. Children deserve attention from both parents, yet this generation into 2020 does not specifically consider that anymore.

First, we will view the divorce rate; it has increased over the years. That leaves one parent to care for the child or children.

I'm speaking from experience. This is now– a one parent world-. My first husband divorced me, and I was left one parent with our child to raise. Likewise, my daughter got divorce and had to care for her son – isn't this example – a one parent world. It is up to our court system who the children will go to, but God ordained two parents. It takes male and female engaged in sex reproduction, to form a fetus, egg and sperm connection in the uterus.

Upon marriage we say we belong together; why separate? Here are a few reasons why we must stay together. We must love one another as God loves us. To become one in marriage is a real serious decision. The child or children have part of both parents alike. Why is this world of adults not obeying God? He gave us two different bodies – female ovaries – male testicles – once reproduction takes place. Because of simulation we form children we love.

It takes two to conceive, it becomes hard when the parents don't stay together. Why is it a one parent world? The blessings come from God. How can we be mistaken, when we think we will be bless raising our children by ourselves? People are going to "sperm" banks, and likewise being one parent, without having Blessings from God. Most of the time, their lives will be shorter. He may bear our griefs and carry our sorrows. Yet we become afflicted, and it hurts our uprisings. Our children are our heritage; family and friends we must stay together. It is harder for one parent to get over infirmities and sicknesses, than two praying together. Have mercy on us, God. Bless one, Bless one another.

My advice is I'm truly Blessed being a one parent, with education from two different university of two different states. My children are adults and are doing well and are educated.

God has power to work with a relationship; we must allow Him to do so. He can work miracles; a couple that prays together stays together. That is an old saying, but is wise in believing.

To live alone, I mean without your spouse, taking care of a child or children is hard, but certainly not impossible. Using me as an example again, my source of help I can surely say was God, without Him I would not have made it this far. Ya, it's a one parent world. God will do what he said he will do. He will protect and guide even a single parent. Just think he will do for two. In a one – union marriage. At the wedding it is said, these two shall become one when united.

The sense of fertility is mighty through God. When a woman becomes fertile her body is no longer her own. Her male companion is now a part of her; because a new human being is now a formed fetus who will someday be born to both of them. Whether or not the child is raised by both parents has become a decision made along the way. Nowadays, what the future holds is a one parent world. To stay together after marriage or to be separated after conception is subject to be considered. Why be called mom and dad if you are not going to live it. God have mercy on us. I'm a witness to a one parent world, because God has given me peace about my situation.

Yes, there are less marriages today than ever before. Why get married if you are not going to raise your children together? I think the object of having happy kids is in unity with both parents.

We must bring everything to God in prayer. By His Grace, I have sustained my life without my husband; it has not been easy, but through His miracles, I've become above and not beneath; strong and not weak.

If you are a one parent, let me encourage you: stay in the Bible. It will give you inspirational direction. Pray for another partner, then you and him can become two parents again. Yes, oh yes, it is a one parent world. This essay is to reveal.

I said I do?
"But."
To Be or not To Be?
Get married, Stay married!!

FAMILY COLLAGE

Verler LaGrange Robertson Gordon (2021)

Verler and her oldest son, Jackie Robertson, Jr.

Verler and her daughter, Ranada Gordon
(2016 LaGrange Family Reunion)

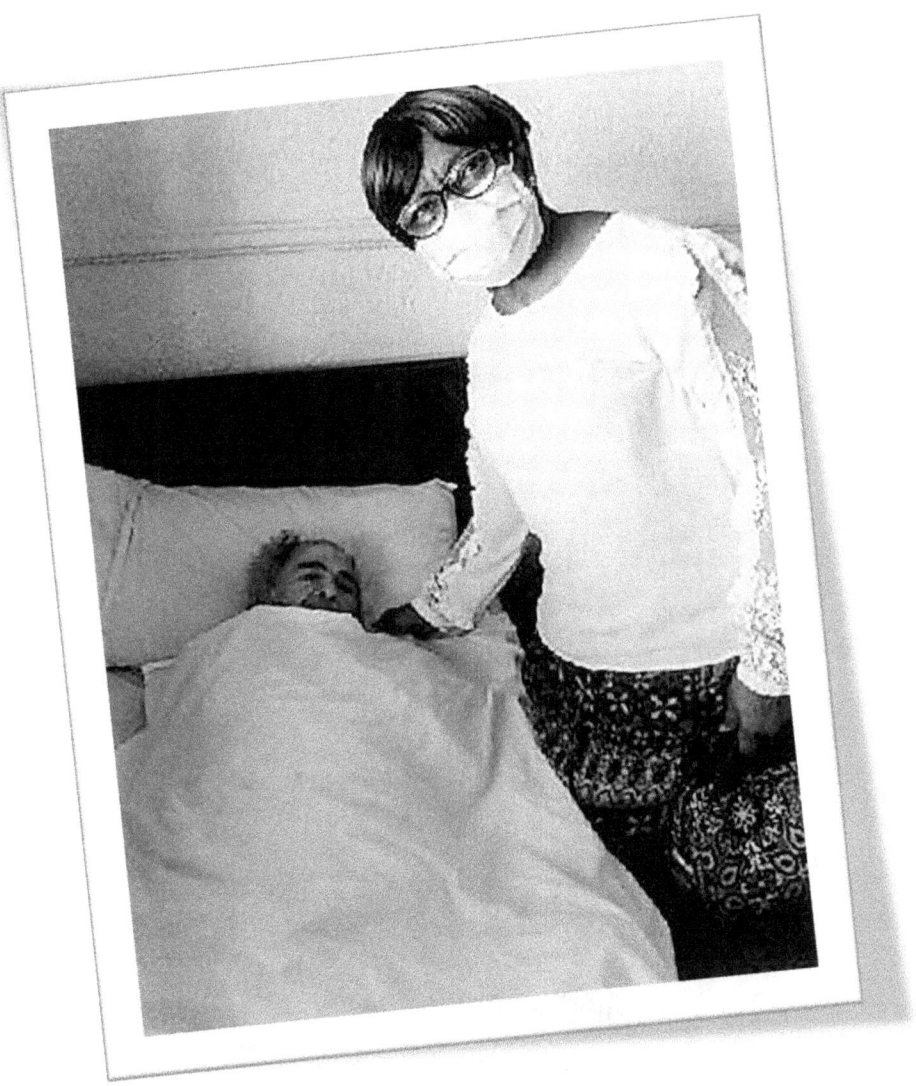

Verler and her husband, Russell Gordon (2020)

Lance Gordon (son) and his
baby girl, Ava Gordon (July 2020)

Top: Verler and daughter-in-law, Magan Gordon
Right Side: Verler and granddaughter, Amiree Boyd

Bottom: Grandsons, Camron Gordon and Micah Gordon (2020)
Right Side: Family portrait drawn by grandson, Camron Gordon

Top: Wedding: Leopold LaGrange (dad), Russell Gordon, Verler, and Elvina Noel LaGrange (mom)

Bottom: Mom and Dad with brother, Paul LaGrange

Top: Verler and sisters: Marie Broussard, Dorothy James, Rose Floyd, Verler, Marie Espree, Barbara Offord (2019)

Bottom: Verler and siblings: Verler, Marie Espree, Rose Floyd, Andrew LaGrange, Marie Broussard, Redella Cousins, Dorothy James, Mary Batiste

ACKNOWLEDGEMENTS

*He has put a new song in my mouth—
Praise to our God;
Many will see it and fear,
And will trust in the LORD.*

Psalm 40:3 (NKJV)

First, and far most I begin by giving thanks to the Almighty God for entrusting in me the spirit of revelations through daily messages and for using me as an instrument to bring forth the deliverance of these gospel songs.

A special recognition to my deceased parents: the late Leopold LaGrange and Elvina Noel LaGrange, who breathe life into me with instilled faith showed me how to accomplish my dreams through the power of storytelling.

Thanks to my wonderful sister Dorothy LaGrange James, for the beautiful Foreword describing my journey using Psalms 54 and my obedience to the Lord to transcend these gospel songs.

Special thanks to Byron Broussard, my nephew and author of "An Ode to Perception and Awareness: Perspective Through Persons." Byron was my driver after my visits to his mom's house. *As commonly said: "association brings on assimilation."* He was instrumental in converting my handwritten poems, songs, essays, and biography to electronic format.

Thanks to my beloved sister, Rose LaGrange Floyd who was instrumental in converting some of my handwritten script into digital documents. Thanks Rose for organizing the book review meetings and working directly with Heavenly Realm Publishing and their Author Advisor Team.

Special thanks to Joyce (Morale) Robertson, our beloved cousin and author of "The Biography of a Woman Who 'Did it All' Clara (Morale) Broussard." Joyce introduced us to Heavenly Realm Publishing.

Thanks to my children Jackie Robertson, Ranada Caesar, and Lance Gordon for being a part of the book committee and for their efforts during the book reviews and for their contributions to my book.

Thanks to my sisters Marie Broussard, Marie Espree, Barbara Offord, and Mary Batiste, who always extended a lending ear and open heart. A special thanks to my brother Marine Lance Corporal Andrew LaGrange, veteran of the Vietnam War. I will forever be in his grace.

A warm thanks to the Gordon family members for taking care of my husband Joseph Russell Gordon who resided in a nursing home while this gospel song book was conceived.

Lastly, thanks to my deceased brother Paul LaGrange and sister Redella Pete Cousins, and to my nephew DeMarcus LaGrange, and my niece Kimberly James Coleman—all lives cut short. They were the trailblazers and entrepreneurs of the LaGrange family who left their mark for humanity.

I am forever grateful to everyone for their support and dedication and for believing in me. To **God** be the **glory** for all he has done!

Sing to the LORD, bless His name;
Proclaim the good news of His salvation from day to day.
Psalm 96:2 (NKJV)

MEET THE AUTHOR

Verler LaGrange Robertson Gordon

*"Seek ye the Lord while he may be found,
call ye upon him while he is near" Isa. 55:6 (KJV).*

Verler Gordon is a two-time cancer survivor who at the young age of 23 was diagnosed with Manic-depression and Schizophrenia. Consequently, she had a roller-coaster life with bouts of mental illness, visits in and out of hospitals/assisted living facilities, and sexual abuse. By the grace of God, she successfully raised three children into full-functioning adults. She has a beautiful mind of high intelligence with strong memory recall. Her heart is made of love—love for family, love for learning, love for giving, and love for her Lord and Savior, **Jesus Christ.**

Inspired by God and the power of his holy spirit, she wrote this book of gospel songs. Through obedience to Him, she was healed and now lives happily in Lafayette, Louisiana.

www.ingramcontent.com/pod-product-compliance
Lightning Source LLC
Chambersburg PA
CBHW070528100426
42743CB00010B/1993